Yes, They Are Real.

Unicorns of the Magical World

Unicorns live in the magical world, and the magical world is visible only to those who believe in magic. Unicorns may wander into your dreams as you sleep, or even show up in your garden when you practice your magic arts, cast spells, or make potions. In my family, we believe in magic, and welcome magical creatures. But most people know about unicorns only from legends and ancient books. Their ideas are often far from reality!

In this book we'll learn what people have known about unicorns throughout history. You will read some very strange stories and understand why many grownups pretend they don't believe in unicorns, even if they do.

A History Timeline

A unicorn as we know it, is an animal looking like a horse with a straight spiraling horn on its forehead. Unicorns are gentle, playful, and fearless. They often appear to people to offer help or friendship.

Let's dive into ancient history to find out where people who had no idea about real magical unicorns got their bizarre stories and legends. We will use this timeline to trace people's ideas about unicorns:

- Ancient times - 3000 B.C. - A.D. 500

- Dark Ages - A.D. 500-1000

- Middle Ages - A.D. 1000-1300

- Renaissance - A.D. 1300-1715

- Age of Reason - A.D. 1715-1789

- Modern Times

Our calendars use terms B.C. and A.D. to divide the history timeline into two parts: before and after the birth of Jesus Christ.
B.C. = Before Christ
A.D. = *Anno Domini* (*Year of our Lord* in Latin, which means after the birth of Jesus Christ).

Ancient India

The first time Europeans heard about a unicorn was in a book called Indika (*On India*) by Ctesias, a Greek scholar of natural history from the 5th century B.C. He wrote that the unicorn was an animal from India which looked like a donkey with a single horn, and could be white, red, or black. Where did he get that idea? There are no legends about unicorns in India. What Ctesias saw was probably an ancient Indian seal like this showing a bull standing in profile (seen from the side). Ancient artists didn't use perspective, so on these seals it looks like the bull has only one horn.

Photo by Royroydeb

What is perspective? The word Perspective comes from Latin: *perspicere = to see through*. Perspective is drawing things in a way that makes them look real. For example, things that are farther from you look smaller, so you draw them smaller. Compare these pictures - with and without the use of perspective.

Ancient Persia

Ctesias wrote about unicorns when he lived in Persia (old name for Iran) where he worked as a doctor at the court of Persian King Darius II. Persia ruled over Northern India. Ctesias talked to merchants who visited India. He saw things they brought from there. Did he travel to India himself? NO! Yet he wrote a book about it! And guess what he saw in the ancient capital of Persia, Persepolis, where he lived? Look! A <u>winged bull sculpture!</u>
One horn, or 2 horns in profile?
One wing, or 2 wings in profile?

So from then on, people in Europe were always confused about whether unicorns looked like horses, cows, donkeys, or even goats! Thank you Ctesias!

Unicorns are ...Goats?

Here are pictures from old books, showing a unicorn with the hooves, body, beard, and fur of a goat!

Fortunately, some people got it right! The seal of the Russian Tsar Ivan the Terrible shows a unicorn as a horse. But wait a minute, it has the tail of a lion!

Alexander the Great

Alexander the Great was a Greek King and a great conqueror of the ancient world. He lived in the 3rd century B.C. One of the most famous stories about him is how he tamed his horse, Bucephalus. The name *Bucephalus* means *bull-headed*. Legends say that Bucephalus was so wild and fierce that Alexander's dad King Philip ordered that criminals who committed murder be thrown into Bucephalus' cage, where Bucephalus killed and ate them!

Soon after the death of Alexander the Great people started collecting stories about his life to tell them to kids and to save them for history. This collection, known as the *Alexander Romance*, says that Bucephalus was not really a horse, but a unicorn!!! The Alexander Romance uses the word *karkadann* for unicorn. *Karkadann* is a Persian word that means *the Lord of the Desert*. It was used for both, a unicorn and a rhinoceros.

This picture from the Middle Ages shows Bucephalus as a unicorn, in a cage with the skulls and bones of eaten criminals!

BUCEPHALUS

Despite the story in *Alexander Romance*, most historians believe Bucephalus wasn't a man-eating unicorn, but a horse. Whew!... So how did Alexander the Great tame Bucephalus? Alexander was only 14 at that time! They say Bucephalus didn't allow anyone to ride him. Finally, Alexander's dad, Philip, told his servants to get rid of Bucephalus, maybe even kill him because he was useless. But Alexander loved him, and was really upset. One day Alexander discovered what was wrong with Bucephalus: The horse was afraid of its shadow! Alexander turned Bucephalus toward the sun, so that he didn't see his shadow. Bucephalus calmed down and let Alexander ride him. He became Alexander's war horse, and many years later, when he was killed in a battle, Alexander named a city he conquered after Bucephalus.

Alexander the Great

Alexander on a coin

Alexander and Bucephalus

Ancient Rome

Julius Caesar, one of the most powerful leaders of Ancient Rome, brought an army to conquer Gaul (ancient France) around 50 B.C. Caesar wrote 7 books - *The Gallic Wars* - about his 7 years in Gaul.
In one of the books he talks about the ancient Hercynian Forest (Hercynian = oak forest) which grew across ancient France and Germany. It was so big, Caesar wrote, that it would take 9 days to cross it from South to North, and over 2 moths to cross it from West to East.
Caesar says that in that forest you could find a huge beast that looked like a deer, with one horn on its forehead, longer and straighter than any horns Romans had ever seen.
Of course, it was a unicorn!

Julius Caesar

A Roman soldier and a unicorn

Ancient Greece

In Greek mythology we find Pegasus, a winged horse, but no unicorns. Why? Because ancient Greeks thought unicorns were real animals from India.

Greek historian Pliny the Elder wrote that there was a very fierce animal called the monoceros (= unicorn in Greek) which had the head of a deer, the feet of an elephant, and the tail of a wild pig, while the rest of its body was like that of a horse... It had a single black horn in the middle of its forehead. Was Pliny talking about a rhinoceros? It lives in Africa, and since nobody in Europe saw it in those days, people were coming up with weird stories about it.

Around the 3rd century A.D. the Greek scholar Philostratus wrote that *In India they make drinking cups from unicorn horns. If you drink from one, you can't be poisoned, you won't fall ill, you won't feel pain if wounded, or be burned by passing through fire.*

Physiologus, a book by an unknown Christian writer from the 3rd century A.D. describes a unicorn sleeping with its head on the lap of a girl, and says that a unicorn can only be captured by a person with a kind, pure, and innocent soul. It compares the unicorn to Jesus Christ, and the girl to his mother, Mary. That's how unicorns became the symbol of kindness and compassion in European culture.

Dark Ages

In the 6th century a Greek merchant from Alexandria called Cosmas Indicopleustes traveled to Ethiopia and saw unicorn statues in the palace of the Ethiopian King. He wrote about the unicorn: *It is impossible to take this ferocious beast alive. All its strength lies in its horn. When somebody is chasing it, it throws itself off a cliff, turns in the air, falls on its horn, and escapes safe and sound.*

Cosma's book gave rise to the idea that unicorns are wild, fierce, and can't be captured. One of the legends based on his book says that a unicorn would rather jump from a mountain to its death than allow hunters to catch it alive.

Believe It Or Not

None of these ancient travelers ever saw a unicorn, but that didn't mean unicorns were not real. In those days no one in Europe ever saw an elephant or a lion, but everybody knew they were real. There were stories about creatures even stranger than the unicorn. How about the griffin (half lion - half eagle), the dragon breathing fire, or the basilisk (half rooster - half dragon)?

People believed unicorns lived in faraway lands, in the mountains, liked to be alone, could not be captured alive, and that there were very few of them. It was not suprising to them that nobody had ever seen one!

Griffin

Basilisk

Dragon

Unicorn

Genghis Khan

The Middle Ages saw the rise of the Mongol Empire led by Genghis Khan. From Mongolia, he started an invasion that conquered a lot of Central Asia, China, Persia, and Russia, and was pushing toward Europe and India.

Genghis Khan

In 1206 the army of Genghis Khan conquered Tibet and climbed the mountains overlooking the valleys of India. And then, suddenly, they turned around and went home. Why?

The legend tells us that as Genghis Khan reached the peak of the mountain, an animal with a single horn came out of a cave, stood in front of him and bent its knees three times. It was a unicorn!
Genghis Khan thought about this, and said:
This middle kingdom of India before us is the place where many wise men have been born. What does it mean that this wild animal, that can't even talk, bows before me? Maybe it's the spirit of my father sending me a warning from heaven? Good thinking, Genghis!
So he turned his army around,
and India was saved by a unicorn.

Another version of this legend says that the unicorn appeared before Genghis Khan in the mountain pass called the Iron Gate and said: *You shall step no further. Go back!* Thank you, unicorn!

Unicorns in the Bible

The Bible is the Holy Book of Christianity and Judaism. It describes many historical events that happened in the ancient kingdom of Israel.

The Bible has 2 parts:
1. *The Old Testament* written before Jesus Christ, mostly in Hebrew, the language of ancient Israel,
2. *The New Testament*, all about Jesus Christ and Christian teachings written in Greek after Jesus died.

Emperor Constantine
Photo by Katie Chao and Ben Muessig

In A.D. 319 Roman Emperor Constantine became a Christian, and soon the Bible was translated into Latin, the language of the Roman Empire. The name of one animal from the Old Testament was translated from Hebrew into Latin as *unicorn*. Actually it was *a wild bull*.

That translation was a mistake! But because of that mistake, people of the Dark Ages and Middle Ages believed unicorns lived all over ancient Israel!

A unicorn in a medieval book

Middle Ages - Bestiaries

Bestiaries were books about beasts (any animals) popular in the Middle Ages. Most people in those days lived all their life in the same town or village where they were born, and never traveled.

Their only information about animals in faraway lands came from these bestiaries. However, if you think the writers of bestiaries traveled far and wide, you are wrong! Many of them never traveled and simply wrote down the stories they heard from travelers - business people or soldiers.

Many ideas about what unicorns were like came from those books. Here are some pictures from these *medieval* (from the Middle Ages) bestiaries:

Albertus Magnus

This page is from the book *De Animalibus* (*About Animals* in Latin) by 13th century German philosopher Albertus Magnus. In this book he wrote:

The unicorn is an animal of moderate size in respect of its strength. It is of boxwood color and has cloven hooves. It lives in mountains and deserts and carries a very long horn on its forehead, which it sharpens on rocks and with which it can even pierce an elephant. It needs not fear the hunters.

Bad Ideas

People have always known that unicorns are loyal and noble in spirit. As the Christian faith spread in Europe, the unicorn became the symbol of Jesus' love for his mother, Mary. Artists created drawings and sculptures of Mary with a unicorn, like this one.

Legends said that the unicorn would defend itself against anyone except a person of great kindness, compassion and pure heart. This legend gave rise to a really sad kind of story full of bad ideas. The artists of the Middle Ages started drawing a girl hugging a unicorn, or having a unicorn sleep on her lap, and hunters coming to kill it! So it was a trap!

Excuse me, if you make friends with a unicorn, it falls asleep on your lap, and then you are just sitting there as the hunters come to kill the unicorn, are you really a kind and compassionate girl? Unbelievable. Just makes me angry!

Here is a picture from the Northumberland Bestiary, *The Hunt of the Unicorn*. Close your eyes if you think you might cry!

Well, the good news is, these were just cruel fairy tales, none of these stories is true!

Allegory

Artists and writers often use allegory. Allegory is when you take a story and make it stand for an idea. For example, a lion defeating a snake can be an allegory for the idea that courage and loyalty always win, because the lion is the symbol of courage and a winning spirit, while the snake is a symbol of evil.

The bestiaries of the Middle Ages always named a lion and an elephant as the two main enemies of the unicorn. Why? Maybe these stories were not about real animals? They were allegories. The lion was a symbol of courage, and the elephant was a symbol of strength.
But there were things even more important than courage and strength - kindness, compassion, and love.
That's what the Christian church taught, and people of the Middle Ages came to accept this.
Here is a medieval tapestry showing a fight between a unicorn and a lion. It's an allegory, of course.

Chivalry

Thanks to Christian teachings about compassion and selfless love, people in Medieval Europe started to see kindness, charity, and loyalty as more important than courage, cleverness, power, or riches.

That was huge!

In ancient times people lived by the same rules as cavemen: *Only the strong survive.* This changed in the Middle Ages.

Saving kids from a dragon (like on this painting by Arthur Hughes) was now more important than winning a crown. Giving your warm clothes to a person in need was more heroic than conquering a city. It was a new set of rules for knights and their families.

Rules of Chivalry

Some of these rules said:
- Believe what the church teaches and defend the church.

Remember, the idea that love and kindness are more important than power and riches came to Medieval knights from the Christian church, so they were grateful and loyal to it.

- Respect those who are weaker than you and defend them.
- Love your country.
- Never lie, and always keep your word.
- Be generous (give more than take), and charitable (sacrifice to help other people).
- Always protect Good against Evil, Right against Wrong.

The rules of chivalry also said that a knight must treat any woman with great respect, not in the same way he would treat a man, but with greater respect and politeness.

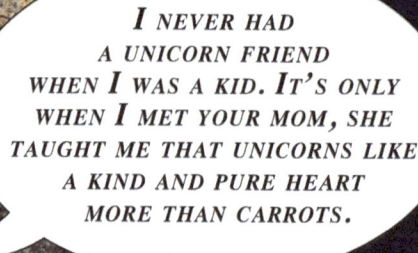

The Accolade by Edmund Leighton

Boys began training to become a knight at age 7 by learning the rules of chivalry. At 12 they started to learn the skills of fighting. At 21 they could become knights in a special ritual, *The Accolade*. A king or a queen tapped your right shoulder, and then your left shoulder with a sword.

LOVE

Chivalry changed people's idea of love. Love became romantic. Stories of knights' tournaments (fighting competitions) tell us that they would put their life in danger to look like a hero in the eyes of a girl they were in love with. This painting shows a knight leaving for war. The lady ties a red scarf around his arm. It was custom, wishing the warrior to come back home soon.

The Lady and the Unicorn

Throughout the Middle Ages the unicorn appeared in allegorical stories as a symbol of compassion, and also of love and loyalty in marriage. Let's look at two such stories, both embroidered on tapestries.

The Lady and the Unicorn is six tapestries woven in Belgium from wool and silk around 1500. The story in the tapestries is an allegory of the 5 senses - sight, hearing, taste, smell, and touch.

SIGHT. The lady is showing the unicorn its reflection in the mirror. This tapestry was probably a wedding gift. The Lady has her hair down, while married women in the Middle Ages always wore their hair up, with ribbons or jewels. Her dress is gold, like wedding gowns of that time.

The Lady and the Unicorn (2)

HEARING. The lady is playing an organ and the animals are listening to the music.

TASTE. The lady is taking candy from a vase to feed a parakeet and a monkey.

The Lady and the Unicorn (3)

SMELL. The lady is making a wreath of flowers. The monkey behind the Lady is smelling a flower it has stolen.

TOUCH. The Lady touches the unicorn's horn.

The Lady and the Unicorn (4)

This last tapestry is about the mysterious 6th sense.
The Lady is standing by a tent that has words
À mon seul désir, in French on it.
It means *My only desire*. What is the 6th sense?
In this allegory, it's probably the sense of right and wrong, or the desire to be loved.
The Lady is returning the jewels which she wore in the other tapestries, into a jewelry box.
What is the meaning of this allegory? Maybe it's that the treasures and riches of the world cannot change your sense of right and wrong... or:
Treasures and riches of the world can't buy love.
The Lion on the tapestries is a symbol of courage and free will, and the Unicorn is the symbol of kindness, compassion, and pure heart.

Mille Fleur

The tapestry style of *The Lady and the Unicorn* is called *Mille Fleur* (mill-flior) = a thousand flowers in French.
The background of the picture is filled with flowers, and these are all real flowers growing in Europe, such as the pansy, lily of the valley, daisy, carnation, and daffodil.
This style was popular for about 150 years around 1500.

Another famous tapestry of that time is *The Hunt of the Unicorn*.

The Hunt of the Unicorn

The Hunt of the Unicorn is 7 tapestries. Hunters attack a unicorn in the woods, kill it, and bring it to a castle where the unicorn comes back to life. Remember, this is an allegory, not a real story!

These tapestries were probably another wedding gift, and the story is an allegory of love.
The unicorn in the woods is the symbol of self-love or selfishness. It is defeated to come back to life as love for family and loyalty in marriage.

In the tapestry below, the hunters find the unicorn in the woods.

The Hunt of the Unicorn (2)

The hunters attack the unicorn.

The unicorn defends itself.

The Hunt of the Unicorn (3)

The last and most famous tapestry in *The Hunt* is *The Unicorn in Captivity*, where the unicorn is alive again, chained to a pomegranate tree, the symbol of marriage.

Coat of Arms

Kings, knights, and noble families of the Middle Ages each had a **COAT OF ARMS**.
A coat of arms is a picture or an emblem that tells us about their family's history. Usually it shows a knight's **SHIELD**, creatures that hold the shield called **SUPPORTERS**, and a **MOTTO**, words (often in Latin) that tell the idea most important to the knight and his family.

For example, here is a coat of arms:
A shield with family symbols, two horses as supporters, and the motto that says *Courage*.

Here is another example. Two dragons hold the shield, and the motto says in Latin *Dei Donum*, which means *God's Gift*.

The art of making family emblems like this was called *heraldic art*.
All the elements of these pictures are *heraldic symbols*.

British Royal Coat of Arms

There were many creatures on the coats of arms of European knights and kings.
- English King Richard III had a lion and a boar;
- Henry VII and Henry VIII had a lion and a dragon;
- Queens Mary and Elizabeth had a lion and a greyhound.

A unicorn appeared on the coat of arms of the kings of Scotland in the 12th century. One horn was seen as a symbol of undivided power. When Scotland and England united, the royal family shield got two animal supporters: A unicorn for Scotland, and a lion for England.
Since the unicorn and the lion were believed to be enemies, the peace between them became a symbol for the unity of the kingdom.

The unicorn is shown bound by a gold chain. As the strongest of all animals, only a gold chain could hold a unicorn in place.

illustration by Sodacan

After a unicorn was added to the British royal coat of arms, it became even more popular in Europe. There is even a nursery rhyme about the lion and the unicorn, which is an allegory for the wars between England and Scotland.

The lion and the unicorn were fighting for the crown;
The lion chased the unicorn all around the town.

Renaissance

Renaissance means *Rebirth* in French. It was a time when the arts and sciences flourished in Europe, and explorers sailed across oceans to discover faraway lands.

Some of the travelers reported seeing unicorns! Jeronimo Lobo traveled from Portugal to Ethiopia in the middle of the 17th century. He wrote:

In the province of Agaus has been seen the Unicorn, that Beast so much talked of and so little known. The amazing swiftness with which this creature runs from one wood into another has given me no opportunity of studying it, but I have seen it so closely that I can give some description of it. The shape is the same as that of a beautiful horse, exact and nicely proportioned, of a bay (brown) color with a black tail. Some have long manes hanging to the ground. They are so shy that they never come out unless other animals are around to defend them.

Wow, that's much closer to a real unicorn than those ancient stories about half-donkey and half-elephant! Good job, Jeronimo!

The Noble Protector

In 1389 John of Hesse, a priest from Utrecht in the Netherlands, went to Palestine, to visit the Holy Land, the places where Jesus Christ was born and lived. Over there, he saw something amazing. Here is what he wrote in a book about his trip:

In the Holy Land, near the field of Helyon there is a river called Marah, the water of which is very bitter. They say snakes poison the water there after sunset, so that the good animals cannot drink of it. But in the morning, after the sunrise, comes the unicorn and dips his horn into the stream, driving the poison from it so that the good animals can drink there during the day. This I have seen myself.

This story is in keeping with many other unicorn legends of those days, saying that the horn of the unicorn disarms poisons, and heals people and animals from wounds and diseases.
Also, the legends about the poisoned river helped the unicorn become the symbol of heroes, noble protectors, like a knight defending a town from an enemy invasion, or saving a princess from a dragon.
Think about it: the lion is so brave, the bear is so strong, the eagle is so royal, but all of them wait by the river for the unicorn to save them from thirst!
Hooray for the unicorn!

Purifying Water

Here are pictures from old books showing the unicorn dip its horn in the river to make the water clean.

This picture is from a 15th-century book on medicine. ➜ Like most art from the Middle Ages and Renaissance, it's an allegory - probably an allegory of marriage. The roses are a symbol of love, and the girl in the picture wears red - the color worn by brides in those days.

Portraits with Unicorns

So now the unicorn became the symbol of kindness, compassion, pure heart, loyalty in love and marriage, and the brave protector of the weak. No other animal was as famous as the unicorn! Everybody wanted to have their picture with a unicorn, but the only way to do that in those days was to have an artist paint your portrait with a unicorn. So many girls had their portraits painted with unicorns. The most famous of them is *Portrait of Young Woman with Unicorn* created around 1505 by one of the greatest painters of the Renaissance, Raphael.

Portraits with Unicorns (2)

Here is another portrait with unicorn, by Italian artist Luca Longhi.

War Horse Fashion

Not only girls of the Renaissance wanted their pictures with a unicorn, boys wanted them too! So the armour that protected the head of a knight's horse from enemy arrows and spears often included a unicorn-like horn!

Unicorn Horn

Sometime in the Middle Ages unicorn horns, called *ALICORN*, started appearing in Europe. Whole horns were very expensive, but the powder made from unicorn horns was cheaper, and it was sold as medicine. Small pieces of alicorn, or alicorn powder cost over ten times their weight in gold. But whole alicorns cost twenty times their weight in gold.

Remember, people of that time believed that the horn of the unicorn could destroy any poison and heal many diseases. Poisoning was a popular way to kill your enemies in Renaissance times. Everybody was afraid of poison. People were making drinking cups of alicorn, hoping that these cups would destroy poison in their drink. Kings of France had a piece of alicorn dipped into their every drink to protect them.

PHOTO: SCIENCE MUSEUM LONDON

Unicorn horn goblet

Testing water with alicorn

Images from Wellcome Collection

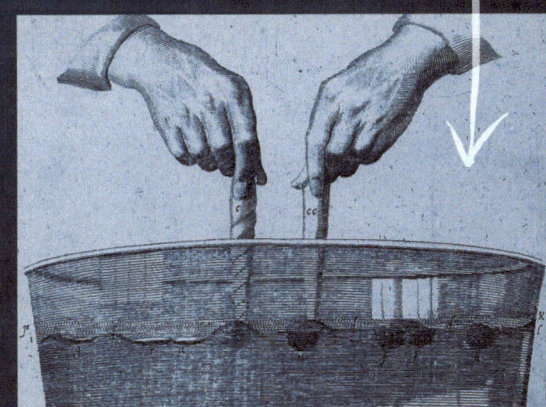

Unicorn Craze!

Pieces of alicorn were fitted into the handles of table knives, carved into spoons, and sold in every pharmacy. There were many strange medicines in those days, like pearls ground into powder, or water with gold dust in it!

So strong was belief in the healing powers of the unicorn horn, that pharmacies in Europe all had a figure of a unicorn over the entrance.

They were also selling alicorn water. What was that? Oh, just water in which someone dipped a unicorn horn!

A unicorn's head pharmacy sign and an alicorn and silver cup for detecting poison from England
Photo: Science Museum, London

The History of Medicines by Pierre Pomet, France

Whole Horns

European Kings and Princes had enough money to buy whole unicorn horns. King Charles VI of France had one. Queen Elizabeth I of England had a unicorn horn she used as a scepter. It cost her 10,000 pounds - the same price you would pay for a castle in her day. Danish kings sat on a throne supported by unicorn horns.

In the beginning of the 17th century Poland invaded Russia, and the Polish army looted the Russian Tsar's palace in Moscow. They captured the royal staff of the Russian Tsar, and one of the looters wrote that *it was made from a whole unicorn horn, all covered in emeralds....It was a treasure more precious than anything in the world ever...*

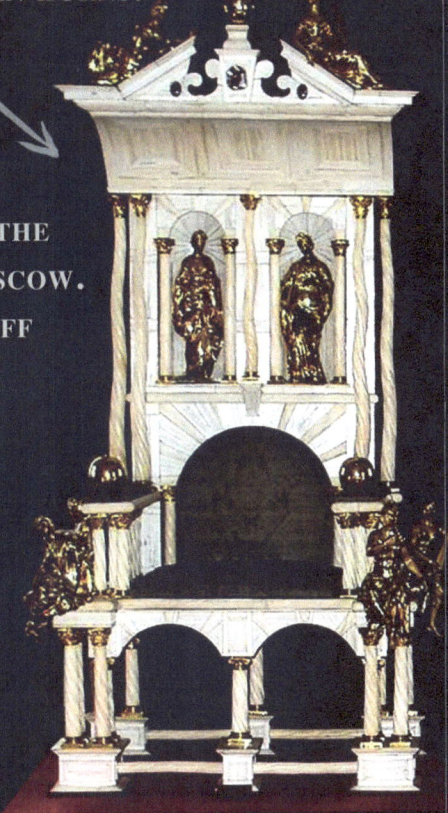

Photo by Sven Rosborn

Were all those unicorn horns real and where did they come from?

To answer this question, let's go back to 10th century Icelend and learn about the life of a Viking explorer Erik the Red.

Erik The Red

Erik the Red was a Viking who sailed from Iceland to the land he called Greenland. He founded the first European village in Greenland.

Erik the Red was born in Norway in 950. When he was 10 his family moved to Iceland. When Erik was 32 he got into a bad fight and it ended in the death of his enemy. A Viking judge made him leave Iceland for 3 years. Erik married his girlfriend, Thjodhild, and moved to an island nearby. But then he got into another fight and the court made him an out-law. In Viking times an out-law was a person who the law would no longer protect, so if anyone wanted to kill him for revenge, it was ok. Erik was scared and decided to go where his enemies couldn't find him.

Iceland

New Land

If you climb Snaefell, Iceland's tallest mountain, you can see a huge island on the horizon. Erik sailed there, and landed on the narrow strip of land that wasn't covered with year-round ice. He called that island Greenland.

For 3 years he lived there hunting narwhals, the whales that live in the northern seas. Narwhals have a straight spiraling tusk (long tooth) coming forward from their mouth.

Viking ship passes an iceberg on its way to Greenland.

Greenland

After 3 years in Greenland Erik the Red returned to Iceland and was met as a hero explorer. In 985, he took 25 ships to Greenland, but after a terrible storm only 15 ships reached the shore. The Vikings built a town there, and continued the narwal hunting started by Eric the Red.

Narwal

As you may have guessed, narwhal tusks were the famous alicorn of Europe! They looked just like unicorn horns.

Narwhals are also found in the Northern seas of Russia, so Russians were selling them to Europe as well. Vikings and Russians may have been honest about the narwhal tusks, because they called them *the horns of sea unicorn*.
Sea unicorn? Seriously? And people believed that?

Yes. In those days they thought that for every kind of animal living on land there is a similar animal living in the ocean:
Horse - sea horse
Lion - sea lion
Unicorn - sea unicorn
Girl - mermaid.
It was only in 1638, that Danish doctor Ole Worm discovered narwhals, and explained to the public that alicorn was narwhal tusk, not unicorn horn. After that the narwhal tusk trade died.

The End of Vikings

Erik's village in Greenland lasted until the 15th century, selling the *sea unicorn* horns. By the way, his son, Leif Erikson, founded the first European town in North America in A.D. 1000.

So where did the Vikings go? What happened to them?

Vikings lived by conquest, gathering riches by plundering the lands they attacked. Then Christianity came to Northern Europe with a strong message that stealing and killing were crimes.

Ingólfr Arnarson, the first Viking in Iceland

Vikings believed that after death you go to the world of the dead where you will need all the things you had when you were alive. This was one of the reasons they were plundering and gathering treasures. When they died, they had all their treasures buried with them, and didn't leave anything to their kids.

But Christians believe that the only thing that matters when you die, is having lived your life as a good and kind person, so they didn't bury any treasures in their graves. Whatever they had, they left to their kids.
As Vikings became Christians they stopped conquering and plundering, and learned chivalry from European knights. And that was the end of the Viking times.

Don't Buy Fakes!

So whole horns people thought were unicorn horns were narwhal tusks. But what they sold as unicorn horn powder in those days wasn't even that. The fake alicorn was made from burnt cow horn, whale bones, clay, bones of dogs and pigs, or from fossils like mammoth or dinosaur bones.

Some writers said that if you take a tusk of an elephant and boil it in water for six hours, it becomes soft so you can bend it and make it straight like a unicorn's horn.
Historian Hector Bothius in his book *History of Scotland* says that Scots hunted walruses, made their tusks straight by boiling them, and sold them in Europe as unicorn horns.

Here is a picture from the book *Fish, Fossil and Fake: Medicinal Unicorn Horn* by Christopher Duffin, London, 1676. It teaches us how to tell the sea unicorn (*Unicornu Marinum*, in Latin) from the real unicorn horn (*Unicornu Verum*).

Test Your Alicorn!

There were many methods to find out if the horn you bought was a real unicorn horn or a fake. Here are some tests to find out if alicorn is real.

Put three or four live and large scorpions into a jar with a piece of alicorn and cover it. If four hours later the scorpions are dead, it's real alicorn!

Throw alicorn into water. If it sends up bubbles that look like pearls, and the water seems to boil, even though it is cold, your alicorn is real!

Draw a circle with an alicorn piece on the floor, and place a spider into that circle. If the spider can't cross the line, your unicorn horn is real!

In 1661, the members of the British Royal Society of scientists put unicorn horn to the test. They made a circle of powdered unicorn's horn and put a spider in the middle. The spider crossed the circle and escaped - the proof that the horn didn't work! Hmmm.... that experiment wasn't very scientific, but I guess they tried their best...
The Royal Society's Latin motto is
Nullius in verba = *Take nobody's word for it*, meaning: Prove it with science!

The Age of Reason?

The Age of Reason, or the Enlightenment, was a time of great scientific discoveries. It was also the time when scientists started seriously studying mammoth and dinosaur bones found in Europe.
In those days people needed to see some bones or skeletons of an animal to believe that it was real. And soon unicorn skeletons started popping up! They discovered 2 skeletons in the Harz Mountains in Germany, and this is, by the way, where Julius Caesar's army saw unicorns!

Unfortnately later these skeletons turned out to be made of mammoth bones and a narwhal tusk.

Here is the picture of one of the fake unicorn skeletons in a book about fossils from 1704.

Unicorn Cave

The place where the fake unicorn skeletons were found in Germany is called Unicorn Cave. They say there was an old wise woman who lived in the woods nearby. She knew medicine, and helped a lot of people, but many thought she was a witch, because she lived all alone in a dark cave near the famous Brocken mountain, where, rumor had it, witches got together to dance and cast spells. One monk heard people saying that she was a witch, and asked the King to send soldiers to arrest her. When he brought the soldiers to her cave in the woods, she walked out, and suddenly a unicorn appeared next to her. The horn of the unicorn was glowing! The unicorn bent its knees, she got on its back and rode away. The monk and the soldiers started chasing her. The soldiers had heavy armor, so they got tired and stopped, but the monk kept running after her. When he was so close to her he could grab her, she lifted her hands up and said a magic spell. The monk fell on the ground and the earth opened to swallow him. The hole in the ground where he disappeared became known as Unicorn Cave.

Tourists from all over Europe come to the Harz Mountains, hoping to see a unicorn. The legend says if you see it, all your wishes will come true.

THE BROCKEN

Brocken is the highest mountain peak in the north of Germany. When the sun is low, the mountain casts scary shadows on the fog and clouds below. In ancient times every year around April 30 Brocken was where a Spring celebration called *Walpurgis Night* was held. People dressed in costumes and made a lot of noise to drive away evil spirits.

After Germany became Christian, people stopped believing in evil spirits, and these celebrations stopped. People started to believe that only witches came to Brocken on Walpurgis Night, and April 30 became known as the *Witches' Sabbath*.

One of the legends about Brocken says that some women secretly come there to ask the Moon Goddess to give them magical beauty, and the Moon Goddess appears to them riding a unicorn!

A witch casts spells
Below:
Witches dance

Looking for Unicorns

As more European travelers went to Asia, Africa and America, they brought more stories about unicorns. In 1720 one traveler reported that in the East of Russia, in Siberia, a hunter had caught a unicorn!

A British soldier, Captain Samuel Turner visited the kingdom of Bhutan in the Himalayan mountains in 1800. The Raja (King) of Bhutan told him he owned a unicorn, and that unicorns are holy animals and you are not allowed to hunt them.

In 1821 another English soldier, Major Barré Latter, while in Tibet, learned about unicorns size of a pony, with hooves like a goat, in the deserts of Northern Tibet. He brought home a black unicorn horn...

1655 book about unicorns by Joannes Jonstonus

They said there was a place in Tibet called Seru-jong which means *village in the land of unicorns*, because local people said unicorns lived there. Russian explorer Nikolay Przhevalsky didn't believe the Tibetans. He wrote *They kept telling us, unicorns are not here, they are over there. Had we gone farther, we would have arrived in India to find a rhinoceros!*

Unicorns in America

Arnoldus Montanus was a 17th century Dutch author who wrote a book about the American continent *The New And Unknown World.*
One of the pictures in the book shows a unicorn. Arnoldus said unicorns lived in North America, somewhere around New York.

Wait a minute, I live in New York and I know we don't have unicorns here...

Unfortunately I don't think we can believe Mr. Montanus. The truth is, he never traveled anywhere beyond Europe.

There you go. Now you understand where all those wrong ideas grownups have about unicorns came from!

If only they had asked kids.
Kids have known the truth all along!

www.ingramcontent.com/pod-product-compliance
Lightning Source LLC
Chambersburg PA
CBHW041504010526
44118CB00001B/19